The Prep-And-Go

Keto Diet Slow Cooker Cookbook

For Rapid Weight Loss And A Healthier Lifestyle

70 Easy And Delicious Ketogenic Diet Crock Pot

Recipes With A Healthy 14-Day Meal Plan

By Roy Larsen

Table of Contents

Introduction

Tired of being fat, sluggish and in a bad mood? Continue reading because this book will open the wonderful world of tasty food to you, and show you an eating style without deprivation. Meals will be tasty for the whole family, so that you would not need to cook one thing for them and a completely different meal for yourself. This book will put an end to your old and unsatisfactory routine, which was a burden to you and to everybody around you. But first things first. Let's start with a brief and crisp summary of what the proposed ketogenic diet is.

Chapter 1 Brief Overview of the Ketogenic Diet

What Is the Ketogenic Diet?

The first official diet with this name dates from the 1920s when it was used therapeutically as a natural and completely drugless treatment for children and diabetics. Later, during the 1990s, it became popular due to Hollywood producer Jim Abrahams using it for his son and promoting its success with the help of Meryl Streep in the 1997 TV movie called *First, Do No Harm*.

Basically, this way of eating limits the daily consumption of carbohydrates from all possible sources to no more than 50 net grams. The lower, the better. The reason for this is to direct our body, in its quest for energy, to replace the use of carbohydrates with the ketones produced by the liver.

When you are on a ketogenic diet, you eat low carb and high fat food. By eating that kind of food, your body will be in a state of *Ketosis*. When in ketosis, your liver will produce ketones which are transformed by fats in your body. That means your body will use fats as your fuel source, then your fats will be burned quickly until you reach your fat loss goal. Usually our number one fuel source is from carbs, but if we are overweight, we want to burn our fats. Then we can follow a ketogenic diet, eating low carb and high fat food, so that our fats will be the fuel source and be reduced day by day.

The main volume of the meals in this book consists of different vegetables, fats, proteins, minerals, and vitamins. The purpose of our book is to translate all this in practical terms, so please, keep reading.

Different Ketogenic Diets

Perhaps names like Standard Ketogenic Diet, or Targeted Ketogenic Diet, or Cyclical Ketogenic Diet sound somewhat familiar to you but you never really explored the subject. Well, there are different types of ketogenic diets. And they serve a different purpose. We will concern ourselves with the diet which is meant to help you with fast and sustainable weight loss – the Standard Ketogenic Diet.

Note of caution: If you have medical issues, such as type 2 diabetes or high blood pressure, it is advisable to work closely with your medical care provider right from the beginning of the diet.

The Health Benefits of a Ketogenic Diet

You **lose weight fast.**

You **have stable energy** levels.

You **become smarter** by increasing your mental focus and clearing your mental fog.

You enjoy **increased endurance.**

You **don't feel hunger** any more.

You **improve your blood profile** indicators.

You **reduce or eliminate** your diabetic medications.

You **regulate your blood pressure** without medication.

You **get rid of** your insulin resistance.

Why Can the Ketogenic Diet Make You Lose Weight Fast?

As we mentioned before, when on a ketogenic diet, your body is running mainly on fat, and this is the fat stored all over you, visible and invisible. This is the fat you want to get rid of and the ketogenic diet is the key for burning it by yourself. The process is pretty simple and straightforward: when you don't supply the usual fuel, the carbohydrates, your smart body uses as an energy source what it already has stored – the fat. Then your fat will be burned quickly.

Important Tips for a Successful Ketogenic Journey

1. Keep in mind that your body needs about two weeks to adjust itself to a new eating style and be patient. The results *will* come.

2. Although you can dine out and still keep this way of eating, it will be much easier if you prepare most of your own foods at home, and this cookbook will help you to do it brilliantly.

3. You will not be as hungry as the carbs are what spikes your hunger but you need to eat your food, even if you are not hungry.

4. At the same time, you don't need to count calories or points.

5. Prepare yourself mentally for the diet by educating yourself well in advance.

6. Get rid of undesirable food temptations.

7. Stock your kitchen well with the desirable products.

8. Supply your kitchen with the tools you need to prepare delicious meals.

Foods Avoided/ Foods Allowed

Avoided

Wheat, Rye, Rice, Potatoes

Sugar, Bread, Sweets, Cakes

Milk, Cereals, Pasta, Beans

Oats, Peas, Parsnips

Corn, Processed sausages

Hot dogs, Honey,Carrots

Beer, Sweet liquor, Soda

Fruit juice, Fruits, Dried fruits

High-fructose corn syrup

Pistachio, Cashew, Candy bars

Aspartame, Diet Soda, Lattes

Ice Cream, Jello with sugar

Jello with aspartame

Milk chocolate

White chocolate

Allowed

Meat, Fish, Eggs, Cheese, Butter, Lard

Cream and sour cream, Olive oil

Coconut oil, Cold pressed oils, Avocados

Nuts – almonds, walnuts, Sunflower seeds

Pumpkin seeds, Flax, chia seeds, Zucchini

Celery, Squash, Cabbage, Broccoli

Cauliflower, Brussels sprouts, Green beans

Kale, Spinach, Lettuce, Cucumber

Tomatoes, Eggplant, Onions

Peppers, Mushrooms,

Berries, Water

Tea and black coffee

Dry wines

Dark chocolate 70% cocoa

Stevia, Erythritol, Swerve

Tips for Eating Out

When you are eating out, choose foods from the right side of the list above. Don't overdo the protein foods, even if they are allowed.

Chapter 2: Everything about the Crock-Pot

What is a Crock-Pot?

If you read the title of this book carefully, you already know that in it, the ketogenic eating style is combined with cooking methods involving a crock-pot or slow cooker, as it is sometimes called. This is a modern spin of the old classic slow cooker, which our grandmothers were putting in the oven. The crock pots or slow cookers of today consist of an independent heating source, housing a ceramic cooking pot – the crock – usually separated from the heating base (in some models you cannot separate the pot from the base) and a glass or ceramic lid. Very important also are the controls on the outside of the cooker. Despite the name, the cooking can be done not only in slow (the experts call it low setting) speed but also in moderate and high speed, depending on the products used and the type of the meal. And guess what? The meals cooked this way are very tasty and moist, with fully blended flavors and mouth-watering aromas – exactly like the ones our grannies were making.

What Benefits Can You Get from a Crock-Pot?

The main benefits are the extremely tasty and healthy meals coming out of this crock-pot. But this is not all. The crock-pot gives you extra time to do your favorite things, to catch up with a friend, to take a walk with someone you love, or simply to relax with a cup of tea and a book. Because you don't need to constantly watch over your meal, there are no spills to clean, no burnt pots, and no baking failures.

Also, you can set the items in the crock-pot in the evening, and when you wake up in the morning, your breakfast will be ready and waiting for you. Or, maybe not your breakfast but your home-cooked office lunch, or maybe your Sunday brunch, or your picnic take-away… Or, maybe you prepared everything in the evening and put it in the fridge; then in the morning you took out the dish to return to room temperature during your morning routine; then you started the timer and left for work or errands etc. And when you came home in the afternoon or in the evening – voilà! As if by a magic, your tasty meal is ready for your family or guests to enjoy.

Types of Crock-Pots Available

There are many crock-pots out there waiting for you to purchase them. Think mainly about the size and the price. How many mouths will you feed? How much money are you able to spend? A good-sized crock-pot is somewhere between 4.5-6 liters or quarts. It will prepare a meal for four to six people. The recipes in this book are calculated for an appliance within this range. Of course, you can buy a more expensive appliance. There are crock-pots of various sizes available. There are two main types of crock-pots: the *digital, or automatic, one*–with all digital controls and a timer, and a lot of other features; and the *manual one*–with nothing more than an on/off switch, and you operate it by yourself. Some more sophisticated models allow you to perform the prep steps in the same pot, where you will make the whole dish. However, you can always do this preparation stage on the stove. It usually takes no more than 5 minutes.

Your crock-pot usually comes with good specific instructions from the manufacturer, but a basic safety rule of thumb is to **never fill it *more than* three-quarters of its volume and never use it with *less than* approximately half of its volume full.**

Some brand names you can get on Amazon are:

Crock-pot SCCPVS642-S Choose-A-Crock Programmable Slow Cooker, 6 quart/4 quart/2 x 1.5 quart – about $132. The price is high but you get three different sizes of crocks for your money.

Hamilton Beach Slow Cooker Programmable 5 Quart Set & Forget (33958A) – about $100. It is fully automatic. So, 'set and forget,' until your food is done.

Cuisinart 6.5-Quart Programmable Slow Cooker – about $76. Also automatic.

Westinghouse WSCD701S Professional Stainless Steel Digital Slow Cooker, 7 Quart – about $45. With wrap around technology, which ensures that the base *and* the sides are heated.

Crock-Pot 4-Quart Cook & Carry Slow Cooker (Stainless Steel) – about $40. Good price.

Betty Crocker BC-1544C Slow Cooker with Travel Bag, 5-Quart – about $40. This one is portable. Think about camping.

Crock-Pot SCCPVL600-B Cook 'N Carry Oval Manual Slow Cooker, 6-Quart – about $30. Manual control.

The following link gives you an overview of top crock-pots and slow cookers available:

https://www.thespruce.com/top-crock-pots-and-slow-cookers-3061721

Important Tips for Using a Crock-Pot - Do's and Don'ts

1. Choose your meat carefully – you need cheaper, fattier, tougher cuts of meat, like pork shoulder or chicken thighs, because the lean, expensive cuts tend to become overly dry. Cooking lean chicken should be limited to 5 hours on low.

2. **Avoid opening the lid during the cooking** process. **Every time you peek in the pot, you lose heat and steam.** If you absolutely *must* open the crock-pot, keep the lid off for the shortest possible time.

3. **Be careful when you add wine or other alcohol since alcohol is not reduced as in the stovetop cooking and it can overpower the taste. A clever tip about alcohol is to brown the meat pieces in another pan on the stove and then deglaze the pan with wine, adding the already reduced alcohol and**

caramelised meat juices to the crock-pot before the actual cooking starts.

4. The closer the food is to the heating element, the faster it will cook. So when you start layering your dish, put the root vegetables, along the bottom of the crock-pot.

5. Milk and dairy products tend to break down in high heat, so add them at the end of the cooking process, or after.

6. The broth in the recipes can be home-made, ready-bought, from cubes or substituted with water. The liquid left in the pot after cooking can be reduced on the stovetop and used as gravy.

7. Invest in a food thermometer to check the finished temperature of your food.

Maintenance of a Crock-Pot

1. Always, *always,* do the cleaning, when the appliance is unplugged.

2. Follow the instructions for your model.

3. Clean after each use.

4. Never immerse the base of the crock-pot – the part containing the electric heater – in water.

5. If there are some hardened spills or burnt-ons, use the tips and tricks of the experts:

6. Soak, soak, soak the problem, until it softens and goes away by itself or with only a gentle push.

7. Do not use harsh chemicals; use dish-washing liquid, baking soda and distilled white vinegar, or ammonia.

8 Try to "cook" a mix of baking soda and water for several hours on high setting. Then wash as usual.

Chapter 3 The Recipes

General information about the recipes

All the recipes in this book are clear and easy to follow. The title is descriptive and indicates the main products used in a dish. The subtitle gives information on how many servings you can expect out of the recipe and gives the approximate preparation time and cooking time. The List of Ingredients is made by the order of use of each item and the Directions are given by the order of the individual steps. At the end, you will find some serving suggestions, like an accompanying salad or drink or a side dish. All the recipes can be divided easily or multiplied, and the great majority of them freeze well.

In the nutrition values, C for Carbohydrate, P for Protein, F for Fat.

Breakfast and Brunch Recipes

1. Greek Style Frittata with Spinach and Feta Cheese

Serves 6. Prep time: 10 minutes. Cooking: 3.5-4 hours on low.

List of Ingredients:

2 cups spinach, fresh or frozen

8 eggs, lightly beaten

1 cup plain yogurt

1 small onion, cut in small pieces

2 red roasted peppers, peeled

1 garlic clove, crushed

1 cup feta cheese, crumbled

2 Tablespoons softened butter

2 Tablespoons olive oil

Salt and pepper to taste

1 teaspoon dried oregano

Directions:

1. Sauté the onion and garlic for 5 minutes. Add the spinach, heat for an additional 2 minutes. Let the mixture cool down.

2. Roast the red peppers in a dry pan or under the broiler. Peel them and cut into small pieces. You can use roasted peppers from a jar, but use those without vinegar.

3. In a separate bowl, beat the eggs, yogurt, and seasoning. Combine well.

4. Add the peppers and the onion mixture. Mix again.

5. Crumble the feta cheese with a fork, add it to the frittata.

6. Grease the bottom and sides of the crock-pot with butter. Pour the mixture in.

7. Cover, cook on low for 3.5-4 hours.

Nutritional values per serving: *net C 9g; P 18g; F 25g*

Serve with avocado slices sprinkled with grated Parmesan.

2. Nut & Zucchini Bread

Serves 10. Prep time: 10 minutes. Cooking: 3 hours on high.

List of Ingredients:

2 cups shredded zucchini

½ cup ground walnuts

1 cup ground almonds

1/3 cup coconut flakes

2 teaspoons cinnamon

½ teaspoon baking soda

1 ½ teaspoons baking powder

½ teaspoon salt

3 large eggs

⅓ cup softened coconut oil

1 cup sweetener, Swerve (or suitable substitute)

2 teaspoons vanilla

Directions:

1. Shred the zucchini and ground the walnuts.

2. In a bowl, beat the eggs, oil, sweetener, and vanilla together.

3. Add the dry ingredients to the wet mixture.

4. Fold in the zucchini and walnuts.

5. Pour the batter into a bread pan, which fits inside the crock-pot.

6. Crumble aluminium foil into four balls, place on bottom of the crock-pot and set the pan in the crock-pot with a paper towel on top to absorb the water.

7. Cover, cook on high for 3 hours. Cool, wrap in foil and refrigerate.

Nutritional values per serving: net C 4g; P 5g; F 18g

Serve cold with tea or coffee.

3. Cheese & Cauliflower Bake

Serves 6. Prep time: 5 minutes. Cooking: 4 hours on low.

List of Ingredients:

1 head cauliflower, cut into florets

½ cup cream cheese

¼ cup whipping cream

2 Tablespoons lard (or butter, if you prefer)

1 Tablespoon lard (or butter, if you prefer) to grease the crock-pot

1 teaspoon salt

½ teaspoon fresh ground black pepper

½ cup yellow cheese, Cheddar, shredded

6 slices of bacon, crisped and crumbled

Directions:

1. Grease the crock-pot.

2. Add all the ingredients, except the cheese and the bacon.

3. Cook on low for 3 hours.

4. Open the lid and add cheese. Re-cover, cook for an additional hour.

5. Top with the bacon and serve.

Nutritional values per serving: net C 3g; P 11g; F 25g

Good for brunch with a couple cherry tomatoes and avocado slices.

4. Ham & Cheese Broccoli Brunch Bowl

Serves 6. Prep time: 5 minutes. Cooking: 8 hours on low.

List of Ingredients:

1 medium head of broccoli, chopped small

4 cups vegetable broth

2 Tablespoons olive oil

1 teaspoon mustard seeds, ground

3 garlic cloves, minced

Salt and pepper to taste

2 cups Cheddar cheese, shredded

2 cups ham, cubed

Pinch of paprika

Directions:

1. Add all ingredients to the crock-pot in order of the list.

2. Cover, cook on low for 8 hours.

Nutritional values per serving: *net C 8g; P 25g; F 28g*

Serve with tomato slices and black olives.

5. *Zucchini & Spinach with Bacon*

Serves 6. Prep time: 10 minutes. Cooking: 6 hours on low.

List of Ingredients:

8 slices bacon

1 Tablespoon olive oil

4 medium zucchini, cubed

2 cups baby spinach

1 red onion, diced

6 garlic cloves, sliced thin

1 cup chicken broth

Salt and pepper to taste

Directions:

1. In a pan, heat the olive oil, brown the bacon for 5 minutes. Break it in pieces in the pan.

2. Place remaining ingredients in crock-pot, pour the bacon and fat from pan over the ingredients.

3. Cover, cook on low for 6 hours.

Nutritional values per serving: net C 7g; P 13g; F 12g

Serve as a side dish to any meat.

6. Pepperoni Pizza with Meat Crust

Serves 6. Prep time: 5 minutes. Cooking: 4 hours on low.

List of Ingredients:

2.2. pounds lean ground beef

2 garlic cloves, minced

1 Tablespoon dry, fried onions

Salt and pepper to taste

2 cups shredded mozzarella

1 ¾ cup sugarless ready-made pizza sauce

2 cups shredded yellow cheese, Cheddar

½ cup sliced pepperoni

Directions:

1. In a pan, brown the beef with the seasoning together.

2. Mix the beef with the cheese.

3. Butter the crock-pot and spread the crust out evenly over the bottom.

4. Pour the pizza sauce over the crust and spread evenly.

5. Top with the cheese and arrange the pepperoni slices.

6. Cover, cook on low for 4 hours.

Nutritional values per serving: net C 5g; P 46g; F 70g

Serve with cucumber slices sprinkled with fresh chopped dill, Himalayan salt and olive oil.

7. The Better Quiche Lorraine

Serves 8. Prep time: 5 minutes. Cooking: 4 hours on low.

List of Ingredients:

1 Tablespoon butter

10 eggs, beaten

1 cup heavy cream

1 cup Cheddar cheese, shredded

Pinch fresh ground black pepper

10 strips of bacon, crisped and crumbled

½ cup fresh spinach, chopped

Directions:

1. Butter the crock-pot.

2. In a large bowl, mix all the ingredients, except bacon crumbles.

3. Transfer mixture to the crock-pot, sprinkle bacon on top.

4. Cover, cook on low for 4 hours. (In the last 15 minutes watch carefully, not to overcook it.)

Nutritional values per serving: net C 2g; P 15g; F 28g

Serve with tomato slices sprinkled with fresh chopped parsley, Himalayan salt and olive oil.

8. Spinach & Sausage Pizza

Serves 8. Prep time: 5 minutes. Cooking: 4-6 hours on low.

List of Ingredients:

1 Tablespoon olive oil

1 cup lean ground beef

2 cups spicy pork sausage

2 garlic cloves, minced

1 Tablespoon dry, fried onions

Salt and pepper to taste

1 ¾ cups sugarless ready-made pizza sauce

3 cups fresh spinach

½ cup sliced pepperoni

¼ cup pitted black olives, sliced

¼ cup sun-dried tomatoes, chopped

½ cup spring onions, chopped

3 cups shredded mozzarella

Directions:

1. In a pan, heat the olive oil. Brown the beef, then the pork. Drain the oil off both meats, mix together.

2. Pour the meat in the crock-pot. Spread evenly and press down.

3. Alternate in layers: pizza sauce, toppings, and cheese.

4. Cover and cook on low for 4-6 hours.

<u>*Nutritional values per serving:*</u> *net C 5g; P 30g; F 37g*

Serve with pickles.

---

9. Eggplant & Sausage Bake

Serves 6. Prep time: 10 minutes. Cooking: 4 hours on low.

List of Ingredients:

2 cups eggplant, cubed, salted and drained

1 Tablespoon olive oil

2.2 pounds spicy pork sausage

1 Tablespoon Worcestershire sauce

1 Tablespoon mustard

2 regular cans Italian diced tomatoes

1 jar tomato passata

2 cups mozzarella cheese, shredded

Directions:

1. Grease the crock pot with olive oil.

2. Mix the sausage, Worcestershire sauce, and mustard. Pour the mixture in the crock-pot.

3. Top the meat mixture with eggplant.

4. Pour the tomatoes over the mixture, sprinkle with grated cheese.

5. Cover, cook on low for 4 hours.

Nutritional values per serving: net C 6g; P 15g; F 12g

Enjoy for brunch with avocado slices.

---

10. Three-Cheese Artichoke Hearts Bake

Serves 6. Prep time: 5 minutes. Cooking: 2 hours on high.

List of Ingredients:

1 cup Cheddar cheese, grated

½ cup dry Parmesan cheese

1 cup cream cheese

1 cup spinach, chopped

1 clove of garlic, crushed

1 jar artichoke hearts, chopped

Salt and pepper to taste

Directions:

1. Place all the ingredients in the crock-pot. Mix lightly.

2. Cover, cook on high for 2 hours.

Nutritional values per serving: net C 3g; P 10g; F 10g

Serve with nut crackers and cherry tomatoes.

Lunch Recipes

1. Butcher Style Cabbage Rolls – Pork & Beef Version

Serves 6. Prep time: 20 minutes. Cooking: 8.5 hours on low.

List of Ingredients:

1 large head of white cabbage – 3 pounds

1 ¾ cups beef, chopped in small pieces

1 ¾ cups pork, chopped in small pieces

1 sweet onion, cut into small pieces

1 red bell pepper, cut into small cubes

1 cup mushrooms, chopped small

2 Tablespoons olive oil

1 cup beef broth

½ cup cooking cream

Salt and pepper to taste

1 heaping teaspoon ground cumin

Directions:

1. Cut out the stalk of the cabbage head like a cone shape, place the cabbage in a pot with the hole up, boil some water and pour it over the cabbage. Let it soak in the hot water for 10 minutes. This will soften it considerably and the leaves will separate easily.

2. Chop the meats into small pieces; place them in a mixing bowl.

3. In a pan, heat the olive oil. Sauté the onion, the bell pepper, and the mushrooms

for 5 minutes, cool them in the pan and add to the meats.

4. Add the seasoning, mix well with your hands.

5. Separate 8-10 leaves of cabbage, lay each one flat, cut the thick part of the stalk and stuff the leaf with about 2 tablespoons of meat mixture. Roll and put aside until meat mixture used up.

6. Finely cut the remaining cabbage and place in the crock-pot. Place the prepared cabbage rolls seam-side down, pour the broth and the cream evenly over the cabbage rolls.

7. Cover, cook on low for 8.5 hours.

Nutritional values per serving: net C 17g; P 42g; F 50g

Serve with beef tomatoes cut in rounds and sprinkle with fresh chopped coriander leaves, coarse salt and olive oil.

---

2. One-pot Oriental Lamb

Serves 4. Prep time: 10 minutes. Cooking: 4 hours on high.

List of Ingredients:

3 cups lamb, de-boned and diced

2 Tablespoons almond flower

2 cups fresh spinach

4 small red onions, halved

2 garlic cloves, minced

¼ cup yellow turnip, diced

2 Tablespoons dry sherry

2-3 bay leaves

1 teaspoon hot mustard

¼ teaspoon ground nutmeg

1 teaspoon chopped fresh thyme

1 teaspoon chopped fresh rosemary

5-6 whole pimento berries

1 ⅓ cups broth of your choice – beef, chicken, or lamb

Salt and pepper to taste

8 baby zucchini, halved

2 Tablespoons olive oil

Directions:

1. Preheat the crock-pot on high.

2. Place the lamb in the crock-pot, cover with almond flour. Add the remaining ingredients to crock-pot.

3. Cover, cook on high for 4 hours.

Nutritional values per serving: net C 24g; P 50g; F 57g

Serve with green salad and yogurt dressing and fresh chopped dill.

3. Zucchini Lasagne with Minced Pork

Serves 6. Prep time: 20 minutes. Cooking: 8 hours on low.

List of Ingredients:

4 medium-sized zucchini

1 small onion, diced

1 garlic clove, minced

2 cups lean ground pork, minced

2 regular cans diced Italian tomatoes

2 Tablespoons olive oil

2 cups grated Mozzarella cheese

1 egg

Small bunch of fresh basil or 1 Tablespoon dry basil

Salt and pepper to taste

2 Tablespoons butter to grease crock-pot

Directions:

1. Cut the zucchini lengthwise making 6 slices from each vegetable. Salt and let drain. Discard the liquid.

2. In a pan, heat the olive oil. Sauté the onion and garlic for 5 minutes.

3. Add minced meat and cook for another 5 minutes. Add tomatoes and simmer for another 5 minutes.

4. Add seasoning and mix well. Add basil leaves. Cool slightly.

5. Beat the egg, mix in 1 cup of cheese.

6. Grease the crock-pot with butter and start layering the lasagne. First, the zucchini slices, then a layer of meat mixture, top it with cheese, and repeat. Finish with zucchini and the second cup of cheese.

7. Cover, cook on low for 8 hours.

Nutritional values per serving: net C 10g; P 23g; F 39g

Serve with green salad and vinaigrette dressing – pink Himalayan salt, olive oil and vinegar.

4. Mediterranean Meatloaf

Serves 6-8. Prep time: 10 minutes. Cooking: 6 hours on low + 3 hours on high.

List of Ingredients:

3 cups lean ground pork

2 large eggs

2 small zucchini, shredded and drained

1 red onion, cut small

1 red bell pepper, cut in small cubes

1 cup hard cheese of your preference – Parmesan or Cheddar, shredded

2 Tablespoons olive oil

1 Tablespoon dry oregano

Salt and pepper to taste

Topping:

¼ cup of ketchup

2 Tablespoons shredded cheese

Directions:

1. Place all ingredients, except topping, in a mixing bowl and combine well by hand.

2. Make 4 folded strips of aluminium foil and lay across bottom of crock-pot in a criss-cross pattern.

3. Sprinkle olive oil across the foil, bottom of the crock-pot and sides.

4. Form one meat loaf from meat mixture, place on top of foil grid.

5. Cover, cook on low for 6 hours or on high for 3 hours.

6. Remove the lid, spread the ketchup on top of meatloaf. Sprinkle with cheese, cook for an additional 5 minutes to melt the cheese.

Nutritional values per serving: net C 8g; P 23g; F 39g

Serve with green salad with nuts and basil pesto.

5. Stuffed Bell Peppers Dolma Style

Serves 6. Prep time: 10 minutes. Cooking: 6 hours on low.

List of Ingredients:

1 cup lean ground beef

1 ¾ cup lean ground pork

1 small white onion, diced

6 bell peppers in various colors

1 small head cauliflower

1 small can tomato paste – 28 fl ounces

4 garlic cloves, crushed

2 Tablespoons olive oil

Salt and pepper to taste

1 Tablespoon dried thyme

Directions:

1. Cut off tops of the bell peppers, set aside. Clean inside the peppers.

2. Chop the cauliflower in very small pieces resembling rice grains, place in a mixing bowl.

3. Add the onion, crushed garlic, dried herbs. Combine thoroughly.

4. Add the meats, tomato paste, and seasoning. Mix well with your hands.

5. Sprinkle olive oil along the bottom and sides of the crock-pot.

6. Stuff the bell peppers with the mixture and set them in the crock-pot. Carefully place the top back on each pepper. If you have any meat and cauliflower mixture left, spoon it between the peppers in the crock-pot.

7. Cover, cook on low for 6 hours.

Nutritional values per serving: net C 11g; P 29g; F 37g

Serve with thin cucumber slices, sprinkled with fresh chopped dill, coarse salt, vinegar of your choice and olive oil.

6. Slow BBQ-ish Ribs

Serves 6. Prep time: 5 minutes. Cooking: 8 hours on low.

List of Ingredients:

3 pounds pork ribs

1 Tablespoon of olive oil

1 small can ounces tomato paste – 28 fl ounces

½ cup hot water

½ cup vinegar

6 Tablespoons Worcestershire sauce

4 Tablespoons dry mustard

1 Tablespoon chilli powder

1 heaping teaspoon ground cumin

1 teaspoon powdered Swerve (or suitable substitute)

Salt and pepper to taste

Directions:

1. In a frying pan, heat the olive oil. Brown the ribs on both sides.

2. Add them to the crock-pot.

3. Combine remaining ingredients in a bowl, blend well. Pour over the ribs - coat all sides.

4. Cover, cook on low for 8 hours.

Nutritional values per serving*: net C 14g; P 48g; F 52g*

Serve with avocado cubes marinated in olive oil, salt and fresh chopped dill.

7. *Steak and Salsa*

Serves 6. Prep time: 10 minutes. Cooking: 6-8 hours on low.

List of Ingredients:

2 ½ cups salsa made of:

2 big beef tomatoes, diced

1 Tablespoon olive oil

1 small red onion finely diced

½ bunch of cilantro, chopped

Salt and pepper to taste

2 pounds stewing beef, sliced in strips

2 bell peppers, sliced in strips

1 onion, sliced in semi-circles

4 Tablespoons butter

2 Tablespoons of mixed dry seasoning:

1 teaspoon ground cumin

½ teaspoon sweet paprika

½ teaspoon paprika flakes

1 teaspoon garlic salt

½ teaspoon fresh ground black pepper

Directions:

1. Cover bottom of crock-pot with the salsa.

2. Add remaining ingredients and mix well.

3. Cover, cook on low for 6-8 hours.

Nutritional values per serving: net C 6g; P 38g; F 22g

Serve with green salad and yogurt dressing.

---

8. Beef Pot Roast with Turnips

Serves 6. Prep time: 5 minutes. Cooking: 5 hours on low + 2 hours on low.

List of Ingredients:

3 pounds beef chuck shoulder roast

2 Tablespoons olive oil

1 red onion, cut into small pieces

1 cup beef broth + 2 cups hot water

4 Tablespoons butter

1 teaspoon dry rosemary

1 teaspoon dry thyme

Salt and pepper to taste

5 medium turnips, peeled, cut into strips

Directions:

1. In a frying pan, heat the olive oil. Brown the meat for 2 minutes on each side.

2. Pour the broth and remaining ingredients, without the turnips, in the crock-pot.

3. Cover, cook on low for 5 hours. Take the lid off and quickly add the turnip strips.

4. Re-cover, cook for an additional 2 hours on low, until the turnips are soft.

Nutritional values per serving: net C 13g; P 72g; F 36g

Serve with sour cream and garlic sauce.

9. Chilli Beef Stew

Serves 6. Prep time: 5 minutes. Cooking: 6 hours on high + 2 hours on low.

List of Ingredients:

3 pounds stewing beef, whole

2 cans Italian diced tomatoes

1 cup beef broth

4 Tablespoons butter

1 teaspoon Cayenne pepper

1 Tablespoon Worcestershire sauce

1 teaspoon dry oregano

1 teaspoon dry thyme

Salt and pepper to taste

Directions:

1. Add all the ingredients to the crock-pot, mix well.

2. Cover, cook on high for 6 hours.

3. Break up the beef with a fork, pull apart in the crock-pot.

4. Taste and adjust the seasoning, if needed.

5. Re-cover, cook for an additional 2 hours on low.

Nutritional values per serving: net C 10g; P 62g; F 25g

Serve with cucumber slices sprinkled with fresh chopped dill, coarse salt and olive oil.

---

10. Pork Shoulder Roast

Serves 6. Prep time: 5 minutes. Cooking: 8 hours on low.

List of Ingredients:

3 pounds pork shoulder, whole

1 can Italian diced tomatoes

1 sweet onion, diced

3 garlic cloves, diced

4 Tablespoons lard

1 cup water

1 bay leaf

¼ teaspoon ground cloves

Salt and pepper to taste

Directions:

1. Place meat in crock-pot, pour water and tomatoes over it, so the liquid covers 1/3 of the meat.

2. Add remaining ingredients.

3. Cover, cook on low for 8 hours.

Nutritional values per serving: _net C 10g; P 43g; F 36g_

Serve with avocado slices and grated Parmesan.

11. Easy and Delicious Chicken Stew

Serves 6. Prep time: 5 minutes. Cooking: 5 hours on low.

List of Ingredients:

2.2 pounds chicken thighs, de-boned and cubed

1 cup chicken broth + 1 cup hot water

3 diced celery sticks (approximately 1 ½ cups)

2 cups fresh spinach

1 red onion, diced

2 garlic cloves, minced

1 teaspoon dry oregano

1 teaspoon dry thyme

1 teaspoon dried rosemary

1 cup cooking cream

Salt and pepper to taste

Directions:

1. Add all the ingredients to the crock-pot.

2. Cover, cook on low for 5 hours.

Nutritional values per serving: net C 10g; P 57g; F 51g

Serve with beef tomato slices sprinkled with fresh chopped parsley, Himalayan salt and olive oil.

12. Chilli Con Steak

Serves 6. Prep time: 5 minutes. Cooking: 6 hours on high.

List of Ingredients:

3 pounds beef steak, cubed

1 Tablespoon paprika

½ teaspoon chilli powder

1 teaspoon dried oregano

½ teaspoon ground cumin

Salt and pepper to taste

4 Tablespoons butter

½ cup sliced leeks

2 cups Italian diced tomatoes

1 cup broth, beef

Directions:

1. Place all the ingredients in the crock-pot by order on list.

2. Stir together.

3. Cover, cook on high for 6 hours.

Nutritional values per serving: *net C 9g; P 62g; F 26g*

Serve with avocado slices topped with sour cream and shredded Cheddar cheese.

13. One-Pot Chicken and Green Beans

Serves 6. Prep time: 5 minutes. Cooking: 8 hours on low.

List of Ingredients:

2 cups green beans, trimmed

2 large beef tomatoes, diced

1 red onion, diced

2 garlic cloves, minced

1 bunch chopped fresh dill (around ⅛ cup)

1 lemon, juiced

4 Tablespoons butter

1 cup chicken broth

6 chicken thighs, skin on

Salt and pepper to taste

2 Tablespoons olive oil

Directions:

1. Add all the ingredients to the crock-pot in order on list.

2. Brush chicken thighs with olive oil; season with salt and pepper.

3. Cover, cook on low for 8 hours.

4. When ready, if desired, take the chicken out and crisp it under a broiler for few minutes.

Nutritional values per serving: _net C 14g; P 26g; F 24g_

Serve with avocado slices sprinkled with grated Parmesan cheese.

---

14. Two-Meat Chilli

Serves 6. Prep time: 15 minutes. Cooking: 6 hours on low + 0.5 hours on high.

List of Ingredients:

1 ½ cups lean ground pork sausage meat

1 ¾ cups stewing beef, cubed

2 Tablespoons olive oil

1 bell pepper, sliced

1 white onion, sliced in semi-circles

1 cup beef broth

2 Tablespoons tomato paste

2 Tablespoons sweet paprika

1 teaspoon chilli powder

1 teaspoon cumin

1 teaspoon oregano

Salt and pepper to taste

Directions:

1. In a pan, heat the olive oil. Brown the beef, transfer to the crock-pot.

2. Then, brown the sausage and transfer to crock-pot.

3. In the same pan, sweat the onion and pepper slices for 4-5 minutes, pour over the meat.

4. Add remaining ingredients to crock-pot.

5. Cover, cook on low for 6 hours.

6. Turn to high, remove the lid and let the liquid reduce for 30 minutes.

Nutritional values per serving: net C 10g; P 28g; F 48g

Serve with cucumber slices sprinkled with fresh chopped dill, Himalayan salt, red wine vinegar and olive oil.

15. Slightly addictive Pork Curry

Serves 6. Prep time: 10 minutes. Cooking: 8 hours on low.

List of Ingredients:

2.2 pounds pork shoulder, cubed

1 Tablespoon coconut oil

1 yellow onion, diced

2 garlic cloves, minced

2 Tablespoons tomato paste

1 small can coconut milk – 12 fl ounces

1 cup water

½ cup white wine

1 teaspoon turmeric

1 teaspoon ginger powder

1 teaspoon curry powder

½ teaspoon paprika

Salt and pepper to taste

Directions:

1. In a pan, heat 1 tablespoon olive oil. Sauté the onion and garlic for 2-3 minutes.

2. Add the pork and brown it. Finish with tomato paste.

3. In the crock-pot, mix all remaining ingredients, submerge the meat in the liquid.

4. Cover, cook on low for 8 hours.

Nutritional values per serving: net C 7g; P 30g; F 34g

Serve with sour cream and cucumber cubes sprinkled with fresh chopped dill.

Dinner Recipes

1. Moist and Spicy Pulled Chicken Breast

Serves 8. Prep time: 5 minutes. Cooking: 6 hours on low.

List of Ingredients:

1 teaspoon dry oregano

1 teaspoon dry thyme

1 teaspoon dried rosemary

1 teaspoon garlic powder

1 teaspoon sweet paprika

½ teaspoon chilli powder

Salt and pepper to taste

4 tablespoons butter

5.5 pounds chicken breasts

1 ½ cups ready-made tomato salsa

2 Tablespoons of olive oil

Directions:

1. Mix dry seasoning, sprinkle half on the bottom of crock-pot.

2. Place the chicken breasts over it, sprinkle rest of spices.

3. Pour the salsa over the chicken.

4. Cover, cook on low for 6 hours.

Nutritional values per serving: net C 3g; P 77g; 20F g

Serve over steamed and buttered broccoli florets.

---

2. Whole Roasted Chicken

Serves 6. Prep time: 10 minutes. Cooking: 8 hours on low.

List of Ingredients:

1 whole chicken (approximately 5.5 pounds)

4 garlic cloves

6 small onions

1 Tablespoon olive oil, for rubbing

2 teaspoons salt

2 teaspoons sweet paprika

1 teaspoon Cayenne pepper

1 teaspoon onion powder

1 teaspoon ground thyme

2 teaspoons fresh ground black pepper

4 Tablespoons butter, cut into cubes

Directions:

1. Mix all dry ingredients well.

2. Stuff the chicken belly with garlic and onions.

3. On the bottom of the crock-pot, place four balls of aluminium foil.

4. Set the chicken on top of the balls. Rub it well with olive oil.

5. Cover the chicken with seasoning, drop in butter pieces.

6. Cover, cook on low for 8 hours.

Nutritional values per serving: net C 6g; P 15g; F 40g

Serve with tomato slices sprinkled with fresh chopped parsley, Himalayan salt and olive oil.

---

3. Pot Roast Beef Brisket

Serves 10. Prep time: 5 minutes. Cooking: 12 hours on low.

List of Ingredients:

6.6 pounds beef brisket, whole

2 Tablespoons olive oil

2 Tablespoons apple cider vinegar

1 teaspoon dry oregano

1 teaspoon dry thyme

1 teaspoon dried rosemary

2 Tablespoons paprika

1 teaspoon Cayenne pepper

1 tablespoon salt

1 teaspoon fresh ground black pepper

Directions:

1. In a bowl, mix dry seasoning, add olive oil, apple cider vinegar.

2. Place the meat in the crock-pot, generously coat with seasoning mix.

3. Cover, cook on low for 12 hours.

4. Remove the brisket from the liquid, place on a pan. Sear it under the broiler for 2-4 minutes, watch it carefully so the meat doesn't burn.

5. Cover the meat with foil, let it rest for 1 hour. Slice and serve.

Nutritional values per serving: net C 1g; P 70g; F 54g

Serve with creamed green beans sprinkled with fresh Parmesan cheese.

---

4. Seriously Delicious Lamb Roast

Serves 8. Prep time: 5 minutes. Cooking: 8 hours on low.

List of Ingredients:

12 medium radishes, scrubbed, washed and cut in half

Salt and pepper to taste

1 red onion, diced

2 garlic cloves, minced

1 lamb joint (approximately 4.5 pounds) at room temperature

2 Tablespoons olive oil

1 teaspoon dry oregano

1 teaspoon dry thyme

1 sprig fresh rosemary

4 cups heated broth, your choice

Directions:

1. Place cut radishes along bottom of crock-pot. Season. Add onion and garlic.

2. In a small bowl, combine the herbs and olive oil. Mix until a paste develops.

3. Place the meat on top of radishes. Rub the paste over the surface of the meat.

4. Heat the stock, pour it around the meat.

5. Cover, cook on low for 8 hours. Let it rest for 20 minutes. Slice and serve.

Nutritional values per serving: net C 7g; P 70g; F 38g

Serve with fresh chopped mint wilted in hot water and guacamole sauce.

5. Lamb Provençal

Serves 4. Prep time: 5 minutes. Cooking: 8 hours on low.

List of Ingredients:

2 racks lamb, approximately 2 pounds

1 Tablespoon olive oil

2 Tablespoons fresh rosemary, chopped

1 Tablespoon fresh thyme, chopped

4 garlic cloves, minced

1 teaspoon dry oregano

1 lemon, the zest

1 teaspoon minced fresh ginger

1 cup (Good) red wine

Salt and pepper to taste

Directions:

1. Preheat the crock-pot on low.

2. In a pan, heat 1 tablespoon olive oil. Brown the meat for 2 minutes per side.

3. Mix remaining ingredients in a bowl.

4. Place the lamb in the crock-pot, pour remaining seasoning over meat.

5. Cover, cook on low for 8 hours.

Nutritional values per serving: net C 7g; P 31g; F 36g

Serve with avocado slices sprinkled with Parmesan cheese and black pepper.

6. Greek Style Lamb Shanks

Serves 8. Prep time: 10 minutes. Cooking: 6 hours on medium high.

List of Ingredients:

3 Tablespoons butter

4 lamb shanks, approximately 1 pound each

2 Tablespoons olive oil

8-10 pearl onions

5 garlic cloves, minced

2 beef tomatoes, cubed

¼ cup green olives

4 bay leaves

1 sprig fresh rosemary

1 teaspoon dry thyme

1 teaspoon ground cumin

1 cup fresh spinach

¾ cup hot water

½ cup red wine, Merlot or Cabernet

Salt and pepper to taste

Directions:

1. In a pan, melt the butter, brown the shanks on each side.

2. Remove from pan, add oil, onions, garlic. Cook for 3-4 minutes. Add tomatoes, olives, spices. Stir well. Add liquids and return the meat. Bring to boil for 1 minute.

3. Transfer everything to the crock-pot.

4. Cover, cook on medium-high for 6 hours.

Nutritional values per serving: net C 3g; P 71g; F 53g

Serve with green salad and lemon juice, Himalayan salt and olive oil dressing.

---

7. Homemade Meatballs and Spaghetti Squash

Serves 8. Prep time: 15 minutes. Cooking: 8 hours on low.

List of Ingredients:

1 medium-sized spaghetti squash, washed

1 Tablespoon butter, to grease crock-pot

2.2 pounds lean ground beef

2 garlic cloves

1 red onion, chopped

½ cup almond flour

2 Tablespoons of dry Parmesan cheese

1 egg, beaten

1 teaspoon ground cumin

Salt and pepper to taste

4 cans diced Italian tomatoes

1 small can tomato paste, 28 fl ounces

1 cup hot water

1 red onion, chopped

¼ cup chopped parsley

½ teaspoon each, salt and sugar (optional)

1 bay leaf

Directions:

1. Cut the spaghetti squash in half, scoop out seeds with a spoon.

2. Grease the crock-pot, place both halves open side down in crock-pot.

3. Mix meatball ingredients in a bowl. Form approximately 20 small meatballs.

4. In a pan, heat the olive oil. Brown the meatballs for 2-3 minutes on each side. Transfer to the crock-pot.

5. In the small bowl, add the tomatoes, tomato paste, oil, water, onion and parsley, add ½ teaspoon each of salt and sugar. Mix well.

6. Pour the marinara sauce in the crock-pot *around* the squash halves.

7. Cover, cook on low for 8 hours.

Nutritional values per serving: net C 16g; 32P g; F 25g

Serve with tomato slices sprinkled with fresh chopped parsley, Himalayan salt and olive oil.

8. Beef and Cabbage Roast

Serves 10. Prep time: 10 minutes. Cooking: 7 hours on low + 1 hour on low.

List of Ingredients:

1 red onion, quartered

2 garlic cloves, minced

2-3 stocks celery, diced (approximately 1 cup)

4-6 dry pimento berries

2 bay leaves

5.5 pounds beef brisket (two pieces)

1 teaspoon chilli powder

1 teaspoon ground cumin

2 cups broth, beef + 2 cups hot water

Salt and pepper to taste

1 medium cabbage (approximately 2.2 pounds), cut in half, then quartered

Directions:

1. Add all ingredients, except cabbage, to crock-pot in order of list.

2. Cover, cook on low for 7 hours.

3. Uncover, add the cabbage on top of the stew.

4. Re-cover, cook for 1 additional hour.

Nutritional values per serving: net C 8g; P 42g; F 40g

Serve with nut bread slices and mayonnaise.

9. Simple Chicken Chilli

Serves 8. Prep time: 10 minutes. Cooking: 6 hours on low.

List of Ingredients:

1 Tablespoon butter

1 red onion, sliced

1 bell pepper, sliced

2 garlic cloves, minced

3 pounds boneless chicken thighs

8 slices bacon, chopped

1 teaspoon chilli powder

Salt and pepper to taste

1 cup chicken broth

¼ cup coconut milk

3 Tablespoons tomato paste

Directions:

1. Add all ingredients to the crock-pot, starting with the butter.

2. Cover, cook on low for 6 hours.

3. Shred the chicken with a fork in the crock-pot. Serve.

Nutritional values per serving: *net C 7g; P 41g; F 21g*

Serve with shredded cheese and sour cream.

10. Beef Shoulder in BBQ Sauce

Serves 12. Prep time: 5 minutes. Cooking: 10 hours on low.

List of Ingredients:

8 pounds beef shoulder, whole

1 Tablespoon butter

1 yellow onion, diced

1 garlic bulb, peeled and minced

4 Tablespoons red wine vinegar

2 Tablespoons Worcestershire sauce

4 Tablespoons Swerve (or suitable substitute)

1 Tablespoon mustard

1 teaspoon salt

1 teaspoon fresh ground black pepper

Directions:

1. In a bowl, mix seasoning together. Set aside.

2. In a pan, melt the butter, add the meat. Brown on all sides. Transfer to crock-pot.

3. In the same pan, fry the onion for 2-3 minutes, pour over the meat.

4. Pour in the seasoning.

5. Cover, cook on low for 10 hours.

6. Remove from crock-pot, place on a platter, cover with foil, let it rest for 1 hour.

7. Turn the crock pot on high, reduce the remaining liquid by half and serve with the shredded beef.

Nutritional values per serving: net C 4g; P 75g; F 22g

Serve with creamed green beans, sprinkled with fresh Parmesan cheese.

---

11. Dressed Pork Leg Roast

Serves 14. Prep time: 5 minutes. Cooking: 8 hours on high.

List of Ingredients:

8 pounds pork leg

1 Tablespoon butter

1 yellow onion, sliced

6 garlic cloves, peeled and minced

2 Tablespoons ground cumin

2 Tablespoons ground thyme

2 Tablespoons ground chilli

1 teaspoon salt

1 teaspoon fresh ground black pepper

1 cup hot water

Directions:

1. Butter the crock-pot. Slice criss-crosses along top of pork leg.

2. Arrange onion slices and minced garlic along the bottom of the crock-pot.

3. Place meat on top of vegetables.

4. In a small bowl, mix the herbs. Rub it all over the pork leg.

5. Add the water. Cover, cook on high for 8 hours.

6. Remove from crock pot, place on a platter, cover with foil. Let it rest for 1 hour.

7. Shred the meat and serve.

Nutritional values per serving: net C 0g; P 8g; F 11g

Serve with creamed green beans, sprinkled with fresh Parmesan cheese.

---

12. Rabbit & Mushroom Stew

Serves 6. Prep time: 10 minutes. Cooking: 6 hours on high.

List of Ingredients:

1 rabbit, in portion size pieces

2 cups spicy Spanish sausage, cut in chunks

2 Tablespoons butter, divided

1 red onion, sliced

1 cup button mushrooms, washed and dried

1 teaspoon cayenne pepper

1 teaspoon sweet paprika

1 teaspoon salt

1 teaspoon fresh ground black pepper

1 cup chicken broth+1 cup hot water

Directions:

1. Butter the crock-pot.

2. In a large pan, melt the butter, add the pieces of rabbit, brown on all sides. Transfer to crock-pot.

3. In the same pan, sauté the onions, sausage chunks, and spices for 2-3 minutes. Pour in chicken broth to deglaze the pan, heat on high for 1 minute then pour the mixture over the rabbit.

4. Add the mushrooms. Adjust the seasoning, if needed.

5. Add the water. Cover, cook on high for 6 hours. Serve.

Nutritional values per serving: net C 12g; P 54g; F 38g

Serve with tomato slices, with olive oil and fresh, chopped parsley.

---

13. Italian Spicy Sausage & Bell Peppers

Serves 5. Prep time: 10 minutes. Cooking: 6 hours on low.

List of Ingredients:

2 Tablespoons butter

2 red onions, sliced

4 bell peppers, sliced

2 regular cans Italian tomatoes, diced

2.2 pounds spicy Italian sausage

1 teaspoon dry oregano

1 teaspoon dry thyme

1 teaspoon dry basil

1 teaspoon sweet paprika

1 teaspoon salt

1 teaspoon fresh ground black pepper

Directions:

1. Butter the crock-pot.

2. Add the sliced onions and peppers. Salt.

3. Pour the tomatoes over them. Toss well.

4. Add seasoning. Mix it in.

5. Arrange sausages in middle of the pepper and onion mixture.

6. Add ¼ cup hot water.

7. Cover, cook on low for 6 hours. Serve.

Nutritional values per serving: net C 15g; P 37g; F 61g

Serve with sour cream and fresh, chopped parsley.

14. Chicken in Salsa Verde

Serves 4. Prep time: 10 minutes. Cooking: 6 hours on low.

List of Ingredients:

2.2 pounds chicken breasts

3 bunches parsley, chopped

¾ cup olive oil

¼ cup capers, drained and chopped

3 anchovy fillets

1 lemon, juice and zest

2 garlic cloves, minced

1 teaspoon salt

1 teaspoon fresh ground black pepper

Directions:

1. Place the chicken breasts in the crock-pot.

2. In a blender, combine rest of ingredients, pour over the chicken.

3. Cover, cook on low for 6 hours. Shred with a fork and serve.

Nutritional values per serving: net C 5g; P 37g; F 50g

Serve with nut bread and sour cream.

15. Salmon Poached in White Wine and Lemon

Serves 4. Prep time: 5 minutes. Cooking: 1 hour on low + 1 hour on low.

List of Ingredients:

2 cups water

1 cup cooking wine, white

1 lemon, sliced thin

1 small mild onion, sliced thin

1 bay leaf

1 mixed bunch fresh tarragon, dill, and parsley

2.2 pounds salmon fillet, skin on

1 teaspoon salt

1 teaspoon fresh ground black pepper

Directions:

1. Add all ingredients, except salmon and seasoning, to the crock-pot. Cover, cook on low for 1 hour.

2. Season the salmon, place in the crock-pot skin-side down.

3. Cover, cook on low for another hour. Serve.

Nutritional values per serving: net C 2g; P 50g; F 27g

Serve with fresh lemon slices and mayonnaise.

Soups

1. Mexican Flavor Chicken Soup

Serves 8. Prep time: 5 minutes. Cooking: 8 hours on low.

List of Ingredients:

2.2 pounds chicken thighs, cut in half

2 cups chicken broth

1 ½ cups salsa:

1 regular can diced Italian tomatoes

1 red onion, diced

2 garlic cloves, minced

1 teaspoon chilli powder

1 teaspoon dry oregano

1 teaspoon dry thyme

1 cup shredded cheese, your choice

Salt and pepper to taste

Directions:

1. Add all ingredients to the crock-pot, starting with chicken pieces.

2. Cover, cook on low for 8 hours.

3. Remove the bones, shred the chicken with a fork. Serve.

Nutritional values per serving*: net C 8g; P 60g; F 55g*

Serve with avocado slices sprinkled with Himalayan salt and fresh ground black pepper.

2. Veggie Chicken Soup

Serves 8. Prep time: 15 minutes. Cooking: 6-8 hours on low.

List of Ingredients:

2.2 pounds chicken thighs, de-boned and cubed

1 cup chicken broth + 2 cups hot water

3 celery sticks, diced (approximately 1 ½ cups)

2 zucchini, diced

1 red bell pepper, diced

1 red onion, diced

2 garlic cloves, minced

1 bay leaf

1 teaspoon dried rosemary

Salt and pepper to taste

Directions:

1. Add all ingredients to the crock-pot.

2. Cover, cook on low for 6-8 hours.

Nutritional values per serving: *net C 8g; P 37g; F 23g*

Serve with sour cream.

3. Mediterranean Fisherman One-Pot Meal

Serves 8. Prep time: 5 minutes. Cooking: 4.5 hours on low + 30 min on low.

List of Ingredients:

1 green bell pepper, chopped

1 cup fresh spinach

1 red onion, diced

2 garlic cloves, minced

1 regular can diced Italian tomatoes

2 cups chicken broth

2 Tablespoons tomato paste

1 cup black olives, sliced

1 cup dry white wine

2 bay leaves

1 teaspoon dry basil

¼ teaspoon crushed fennel seeds

1 ¾ cups medium-sized shrimp, peeled

1 ¾ cups cod, cubed

Salt and pepper to taste

Directions:

1. Add all ingredients (except the shrimp and cod) to the crock-pot.

2. Cover, cook on low 4.5 hours.

3. Add the shrimp and cod. Re-cover, cook on low for 30 minutes.

Nutritional values per serving: net C 9g; P 36g; F 25g

Serve with nut bread and butter.

---

4. French Mint-Ball Veggie Soup

Serves 10. Prep time: 15 minutes. Cooking: 6-8 hours on low.

List of Ingredients:

3 cups beef broth

1 medium zucchini, cut into sticks

2 celery sticks, diced (approximately 1 cup)

1 yellow onion, diced

5 garlic cloves, crushed

1 medium tomato, cubed

3 cups ground veal

½ cup Parmesan cheese

1 large egg

½ cup fresh mint, chopped

1 teaspoon dry oregano

1 teaspoon sweet paprika

Salt and pepper to taste

Directions:

1. Preheat crock-pot on low. Add broth, zucchini, celery, onion, tomato.

2. In a mixing bowl, combine meat, cheese, garlic, egg, mint, seasoning, salt and pepper. Mix well. Shape into mini-meatballs (approximately 45).

3. Heat olive oil in a pan, add meatballs. Brown for few minutes on all sides.

4. Add meatballs to the crock-pot. If necessary, add one cup hot water.

5. Cover, cook on low for 6-8 hours.

Nutritional values per serving: net C 11g; P 32g; F 25g

Serve with nut bread and olives.

---

5. Beef Meatball Soup

Serves 8. Prep time: 10 minutes. Cooking: 6 hours on low.

List of Ingredients:

1 red bell pepper, diced

8-10 pearl onions, halved

2 garlic cloves, minced

2 Tablespoons olive oil

3 cups lean ground beef

1 egg

1 teaspoon dry savoury

Salt and pepper to taste

1 cup beef broth + 2 cups hot water

1 cup sour cream

Directions:

1. Preheat crock-pot on low. Add vegetables and olive oil.

2. In a bowl, combine meat, egg, dry savoury, salt and pepper. Mix well and shape into bite-size meatballs (approximately 30).

3. In a pot, boil the broth, add the meatballs and heat for 2 minutes.

4. Add the meatballs, and broth to the crock-pot. If necessary, add ½ cup hot water.

5. Cover, cook on low for 6 hours.

6. Open the lid and ladle out a small amount of liquid, cool it slightly and use to thin the sour cream. Add salt and pepper, if needed, and return the cream mixture to the pot.

7. Stir gently, not to break the meatballs. Serve hot.

Nutritional values per serving: net C 11g; P 27g; F 28g

Serve with basil-olive paste on nut crackers.

6. Moorish Lamb Heart and Liver Soup

Serves 6. Prep time: 5 minutes. Cooking: 10 hours on low.

List of Ingredients:

3 cups lamb hearts and livers, well washed

1 cup lamb meat, cubed

2 cups broth, your choice

2 cups hot water

2 bunches spring onions, diced

1 bunch fresh spearmint, chopped

2 cups fresh spinach

1 teaspoon garlic powder

1 teaspoon dry basil

1 teaspoon sweet paprika

1 teaspoon ground pimento

4 cloves, lightly crushed

½ teaspoon cinnamon

4 Tablespoons of olive oil

Salt and pepper to taste

1 egg

1 cup full-fat Greek yogurt

Directions:

1. Add all ingredients to the crock-pot, except the egg and yogurt.

2. Cover, cook on low for 10 hours.

3. Take out the meaty pieces and into small, bite size pieces. Return to crock-pot.

4. Beat the egg and yogurt together slowly. Ladle in some of the cooked liquid. Stir slowly to combine.

5. Return the mixture to crock-pot. Stir well to combine. Serve.

Nutritional values per serving: net C 12g; P 56g; F48g

Serve with nut bread and butter.

---

7. Superb Oxtail Pot with Broccoli

Serves 8. Prep time: 15 minutes. Cooking: 8-10 hours on low.

List of Ingredients:

3 pounds oxtail, cut into 1 inch pieces (ask your butcher to cut)

2 Tablespoons olive oil

1 red onion, diced

3 garlic cloves, minced

3 inch piece fresh ginger, peeled, thinly sliced

1 regular can Italian diced tomatoes

1 teaspoon ground cardamom

1 teaspoon ground cumin

1 teaspoon ground coriander seeds

½ teaspoon cinnamon

1 ½ teaspoon salt

1 teaspoon fresh ground black pepper

1 cup beef broth + 1 cup hot water

5 small turnips, cubed

1 head of broccoli, chopped

1 cup mushrooms, washed, dried, diced into small pieces

Directions:

1. Preheat crock-pot on low.

2. In a pan, heat the olive oil. Brown the oxtail on all sides. Transfer to the crock-pot.

3. In the same pan, sauté the onions for 5 minutes, once they are translucent, add the garlic and ginger, heat for 1 minute.

4. Pour the onion, garlic, ginger mixture over the oxtail.

5. Add the remaining ingredients to the same browning pan, bring to a boil.

6. Once hot, pour the sauce in the crock-pot, stir well. The liquid should cover everything. If necessary, add ½ cup hot water.

7. Cover, cook on low for 8-10 hours.

Nutritional values per serving: net C 14g; P 68g; F 39g

Serve with nut bread and butter.

8. Chicken Mushroom Soup

Serves 8. Prep time: 5 minutes. Cooking: 6 hours on low + 1 hour on low.

List of Ingredients:

3 cups chicken breasts, diced

1 cup chicken broth + 2 cups hot water

2 Tablespoons butter

1 regular can diced Italian tomatoes

2 red bell peppers, sliced

1 red onion, diced

¾ cup mushrooms, washed, dried, sliced

4 cloves garlic, minced

1 teaspoon dried oregano

1 teaspoon ground cumin

Salt and pepper to taste

Topping:

2 Tablespoons chopped fresh parsley

Directions:

1. Pre-heat the crock-pot on low. Add all ingredients to the crock-pot.

2. Cover, cook on low for 6 hours.

3. Break up chicken with a fork. Re-cover, cook an additional hour until ready.

4. Serve warm. Sprinkle with fresh parsley.

Nutritional values per serving: net C 4g; P 12g; F 8g

Serve with sour cream.

---

9. Chilli Con Turkey Soup

Serves 8. Prep time: 10 minutes. Cooking: 6 hours on low.

List of Ingredients:

2.2 pounds ground turkey

2 Tablespoons butter

1 red onion, diced

2 garlic cloves, minced

1 cup celery, diced

1 teaspoon chilli powder

1 teaspoon dry oregano

1 teaspoon dry thyme

1 teaspoon of dry basil

1 teaspoon of ground cumin

2 regular cans Italian diced tomatoes

14 fl ounce jar tomato passata

1 cup chicken broth

Salt and pepper to taste

Directions:

1. In a pan, melt the butter. Add the diced onion, sauté for 2 minutes then add the ground turkey, cook thoroughly.

2. Add the vegetables and spices. Stir and cook the mixture for an additional 2 minutes.

3. Transfer the mixture to the crock-pot.

4. Pour the tomatoes and broth over the mixture and stir.

5. Cover, cook on low for 6 hours.

Nutritional values per serving: *net C 10g; P 32g; F 19g*

Serve with avocado slices and fried, crumbled bacon.

---

10. Zuppa Toscana

Serves 10. Prep time: 10 minutes. Cooking: 8 hours on low + 4 hours on high.

List of Ingredients:

3 cups spicy Italian sausage

1 Tablespoon olive oil

1 red onion, diced

3 garlic cloves, minced

3 cups chicken broth

1 head cauliflower, cut in florets

3 cups baby spinach leaves

1 teaspoon sweet paprika

Salt and pepper to taste

½ cup full-fat cream

Directions:

1. In a pan, brown the sausage for 2 minutes. Add the onion, and garlic, sauté for an additional 3 minutes.

2. Transfer mixture to the crock-pot.

3. Add the remaining ingredients (except the cream). Stir well.

4. Cover, cook on low for 8 hours or on high for 4 hours.

5. Stir in the cream and serve hot.

Nutritional values per serving: *net C 7g; P 14g; F 19g*

Serve with bacon bread slices.

Nut Breads and Side Dishes

1. Garlicky Mashed Cauliflower

Serves 6. Prep time: 10 minutes. Cooking: 3 hours on high.

List of Ingredients:

1 good-sized head of cauliflower, cut into florets

1 small head of garlic, peeled

4 cups vegetable broth

3 Tablespoons of butter

⅓ cup sour cream

4 Tablespoons combined fresh chopped herbs: chives, parsley or spring onions

Salt and pepper

Directions:

1. Place the cauliflower, garlic in the crock-pot. Pour in broth until cauliflower is covered. Add more liquid, if needed.

2. Cover, cook on high for 3 hours.

3. Drain the liquid, reserving for later.

4. Mash the vegetables with a fork or a potato masher.

5. Add the cream and butter and mash again until smooth. If necessary, add some of the reserved cooking liquid to soften the mash.

6. Mix in chopped herbs, add salt and fresh ground pepper. Stir to combine thoroughly.

Nutritional values per serving: net C 7g; P 13g; F 6g

Serve warm to accompany roasted meats.

---

2. Brussels Sprouts Au Gratin

Serves 6. Prep time: 5 minutes. Cooking: 6 hours on low.

List of Ingredients:

2.2 pounds Brussels sprouts, washed, dried, trimmed and halved

1 cup cream

Zest of 1 lemon

1 teaspoon black pepper

1 teaspoon salt

4 Tablespoons butter

1 cup Parmesan cheese, grated

½ cup almond meal

Salt and pepper to taste

Directions:

1. Butter the crock-pot.

2. Place the trimmed Brussels sprouts in the crock-pot. Sprinkle with seasoning. Pour the cream over the Brussel sprouts. Toss to cover them.

3. In a bowl, cut the butter into small pieces. Add ½ cup of the Parmesan cheese,

almond meal, salt and pepper. Stir until combined.

4. Mix with sprouts. Add the remaining Parmesan cheese. Pour over the Brussel sprouts in the crock-pot.

5. Cover, cook on low for 6 hours.

Nutritional values per serving: net C 5g; P 10g; F 25g

Serve as a side dish to any meat.

---

3. Cauliflower Garlic Bread

Serves 8. Prep time: 10 minutes. Cooking: 4 hours on high.

List of Ingredients:

1 head of cauliflower, cut into florets

2 large eggs

2 cups shredded cheese, your choice

3 Tablespoons coconut flakes

½ teaspoon salt

½ teaspoon fresh ground black pepper

2 cloves garlic, minced

4 Tablespoons fresh basil, coarsely chopped

Directions:

1. Chop the cauliflower to a rice-like consistency. Place in a bowl.

2. Stir in 1 cup cheese, eggs, coconut flakes, salt and pepper. Combine well.

3. Butter bottom of the crock-pot. Press mixture to bottom of the crock-pot to form a crust.

4. Sprinkle with garlic and remaining cheese.

5. Cover, cook on high for 4 hours.

6. Sprinkle with chopped basil.

Nutritional values per serving: net C 2g; P 10g; F 10g

Serve warm.

---

4. Pumpkin Nut Bread

Serves 10. Prep time: 10 minutes. Cooking: 3 hours on low.

List of Ingredients:

1 ½ cup ground almonds (2 cups, if you reduce the sweetener; see below)

¾ cup sweetener, Swerve (½ cup, if you prefer not so sweet breakfast version)

½ cup coconut flour

¼ cup unsweetened whey protein powder

2 teaspoons baking powder

1 ½ teaspoon cinnamon

1 teaspoon turmeric

1 teaspoon ground ginger

¼ teaspoon ground cloves

Pinch of salt

1 cup pumpkin, mashed

4 large eggs

¼ cup butter, melted

1 teaspoon vanilla extract

Directions:

1. Butter the crock-pot.

2. In a bowl, combine the walnuts with dry ingredients.

3. Stir in the pumpkin, eggs, butter, and vanilla. Mix well.

4. Pour the batter in the buttered crock-pot.

5. Cover the crock-pot with a paper towel to absorb the water.

6. Cover, cook on low for 3 hours.

Nutritional values per serving: net C 5g; P 6g; F 13g

Serve with whipped cream and espresso.

5. *Peanut Butter & Chocolate Cake*

Serves 12. Prep time: 10 minutes. Cooking: 4 hours on low.

List of Ingredients:

1 Tablespoon butter for greasing the crock-pot

2 cups almond flour

¾ cup sweetener, your choice

¼ cup coconut flakes

¼ cup whey protein powder

1 teaspoon baking powder

¼ teaspoon salt

¾ cup peanut butter, room temperature

4 large eggs

1 teaspoon vanilla extract

½ cup water

3 Tablespoons sugarless dark chocolate, melted

Directions:

1. Grease the crock-pot well.

2. In a bowl, mix the dry ingredients. One item at a time, stir in the wet ingredients.

3. Spread about 2/3 of batter in the crock-pot, add half the chocolate. Swirl with a fork. Top up with the remaining batter and chocolate. Swirl with fork again.

4. Cover, cook on low for 4 hours. Switch off. Let it set covered for 30 minutes.

Nutritional values per serving: net C 5g; P 6g; F 20g

Serve with whipped cream and espresso.

---

6. Greek Mushroom Stew

Serves 6. Prep time: 5 minutes. Cooking: 4 hours on low.

List of Ingredients:

2.2 pounds button mushrooms, washed and dried

½ cup olive oil

½ cup spring onions, chopped

½ cup black olives rings

1 ½ cup chicken broth

Salt and pepper to taste

Directions:

1. Place the cleaned mushrooms in the crock-pot.

2. Add the remaining ingredients. Stir.

3. Cover, cook on low for 4 hours.

Nutritional values per serving: net C 14g; P 16g; F 20g

Sprinkle with fresh chopped coriander, serve as a side dish to roasted meat.

7. Green Bean Casserole

Serves 8. Prep time: 10 minutes. Cooking: 3 hours on high.

List of Ingredients:

8 bacon strips, crisped and crumbled

1 yellow onion, sliced

2.2 pounds fresh green beans, trimmed

¼ cup chicken broth

Salt and pepper to taste

3 sprigs fresh thyme

Directions:

1. In a pan, fry the bacon. Set aside.

2. In the same pan, add some olive oil, sauté the onion 3-4 minutes. Add the beans, cook for 2 minutes.

3. Transfer to crock-pot, add the remaining ingredients. Stir.

4. Cover, cook on high for 3 hours.

5. Open the lid, sprinkle the crumbled bacon. Serve warm.

Nutritional values per serving: net C 8g; P 9g; F 6g

Sprinkle with fresh chopped coriander, serve as a side dish to roasted meat.

8. *Broccoli & Cauliflower & Blue Cheese Casserole*

Serves 10. Prep time: 15 minutes. Cooking: 6 hours on low.

List of Ingredients:

Alfredo sauce:

4 Tablespoons butter

2 crushed garlic cloves

2 cups heavy cream

½ cup grated Parmesan cheese

Main Dish:

4 cups broccoli florets, fresh or frozen

4 cups cauliflower florets, fresh or frozen

1 red onion, diced

1 teaspoon dry oregano, thyme, or basil

¾ cup any blue cheese, crumbled

Salt and pepper to taste

Directions:

1. In a small pot, combine ingredients for Alfredo sauce. Simmer for 10 minutes.

2. Add remaining ingredients to the crock-pot.

3. Pour the warm Alfredo sauce over mixture in crock-pot.

4. Cover, cook on low for 6 hours.

Nutritional values per serving: *net C 6g; P 9g; 29F g*

Serve as a side dish with tomato slices sprinkled with fresh chopped parsley, Himalayan salt and olive oil.

---

9. Flax Meal Coffeecake

Serves 8. Prep time: 15 minutes. Cooking: 2.5 hours on low.

List of Ingredients:

1 Tablespoon butter for the crock-pot

10 eggs

¾ cup coconut flour

1 tablespoon gelatin

1 cup butter, divided

½ cup flax seed meal

½ teaspoon baking soda

¾ cup powdered Swerve, divided (or suitable substitute)

2 teaspoons vanilla extract, divided

2 teaspoons cinnamon

½ cup of warm water

Directions:

1. Butter the crock-pot.

2. In a blender, mix the eggs, flour, ½ cup butter, sweetener, gelatin and vanilla.

Blend for 20 seconds.

3. In a small bowl, mix flax meal and baking soda. Add to mixture in blender. Blend for 10 seconds.

4. Combine ½ cup melted butter, sweetener, water, and cinnamon to make a syrup; add a bit of water, if not liquid enough.

5. Pour 1 layer of batter in the buttered crock-pot.

6. Sprinkle with ¼ of the syrup.

7. Repeat two more times, finishing with ½ of the syrup.

8. Cover the crock-pot with a paper towel to absorb the water.

9. Cover, cook on low for 2.5 hours.

Nutritional values per serving: net C 4g; P 9g; F 24g

Serve with cream cheese topping.

---

10. Savoury Almond Bread

Serves 8. Prep time: 10 minutes. Cooking: 3 hours on low.

List of Ingredients:

2 cups ground almonds

½ cup flax seed meal

Salt and pepper to taste

½ teaspoon baking soda

2 large eggs

¼ cup basil pesto sauce

¼ cup Parmesan

1 ½ Cheddar cheese, grated

1 cup coconut milk

Directions:

1. Combine dry ingredients in a bowl.

2. Blend wet ingredients in another bowl.

3. Mix the two slowly.

4. Butter the crock-pot, pour in the batter.

5. Cover the crock-pot with a paper towel to absorb the water.

6. Cover, cook on low for 3 hours.

Nutritional values per serving: net C 9g; P 13g; F 28g

Serve as an accompaniment with hearty soup or one-pot meal.

Dessert Recipes

1. Mocha Brownie

Serves 12. Prep time: 15 minutes. Cooking: 3 hours on low.

List of Ingredients:

1 Tablespoon butter for the crock-pot

½ cup butter

½ cup double cream

2 Tablespoons instant coffee

1 Bourbon vanilla pod, scraped

½ teaspoon cinnamon

4 Tablespoons Dutch cocoa powder

⅓ cup ground almonds

Pinch of salt

5 large eggs

⅔ cup granulated Swerve (or suitable substitute)

Directions:

1. Butter the crock-pot.

2. In a small pan, melt the butter and chocolate. Cool.

3. In another bowl, beat the cream, coffee, and vanilla together.

4. Combine the cocoa, almonds, and salt in a bowl.

5. Whisk the eggs and granulated Swerve together for 5 minutes.

6. Slowly add the chocolate mixture to the eggs, beat with a mixer.

7. Stir in the cocoa-almond mix.

8. Slowly add the cream and coffee mixture.

9. Pour the batter in the buttered crock-pot.

10. Cover the pot with a paper towel to absorb the water.

11. Cover, cook on low for 3 hours.

Nutritional values per serving: net C 2g; P 4g; F 14g

Serve with whipped cream and espresso.

---

2. Slim Waist, Rich Taste Chocolate Cake

Serves 12. Prep time: 10 minutes. Cooking: 3 hours on low.

List of Ingredients:

1 ½ cups almond flour

¾ cup granulated or powdered sweetener of your choice

⅔ cup cocoa powder

¼ cup whey protein powder

2 teaspoons baking powder

¼ teaspoon salt

½ cup butter, melted (reserve some to brush the crock-pot)

4 large eggs

¾ unsweetened almond milk

1 teaspoon vanilla extract

Directions:

1. In a bowl, mix the dry ingredients.

2. Stir in the wet ingredients one at a time. Combine thoroughly.

3. Butter the crock-pot. Pour in the cake batter.

4. Cover, cook on low for 3 hours. Switch off. Let it set uncovered for 30 minutes.

Nutritional values per serving: net C 4g; P 8g; F 14g

Serve with whipped cream and espresso.

3. Lemon Cake

Serves 8. Prep time: 10 minutes. Cooking: 3 hours on high.

List of Ingredients:

1 ½ cup ground almonds

½ cup coconut flakes

6 Tablespoons sweetener like Swerve (Erythritol, or suitable substitute)

2 teaspoons baking powder

Pinch of salt

½ cup softened coconut oil

½ cup cooking cream

2 Tablespoons lemon juice

Zest from two lemons

2 eggs

Topping:

3 tablespoons Swerve (or suitable substitute)

½ cup boiling water

2 Tablespoons lemon juice

2 Tablespoons softened coconut oil

Directions:

1. In a bowl, combine the almonds, coconut, sweetener, baking powder. Whisk until combined.

2. In a separate bowl, blend coconut oil, cream, juice, and eggs together.

3. Add the egg mixture to the dry ingredients. Mix thoroughly.

4. Line the crock-pot with aluminium foil, pour in the batter.

5. In a bowl, mix the topping. Pour it over the cake batter.

6. Cover the top of the crock-pot with paper towels to absorb the water.

7. Cover, cook on high for 3 hours. Serve warm.

Nutritional values per serving: _net C 5g; P 7g; F 30g_

Serve with whipped cream and espresso.

4. Raspberry & Coconut Cake

Serves 10. Prep time: 15 minutes. Cooking: 3 hours on low.

List of Ingredients:

2 cups ground almonds

1 cup shredded coconut

¾ cup sweetener, Swerve (or suitable substitute)

2 teaspoon baking soda

¼ teaspoon salt

4 large eggs

½ cup melted coconut oil

¾ cup coconut milk

1 cup raspberries, fresh or frozen

½ cup sugarless dark chocolate chips

Directions:

1. Butter the crock-pot.

2. In a bowl, mix the dry ingredients.

3. Beat in the eggs, melted coconut oil, and coconut milk. Gently fold in the raspberries and chocolate chips.

4. Combine the cocoa, almonds, and salt in a bowl.

5. Pour the batter into the buttered crock-pot.

6. Cover the crock-pot with a paper towel to absorb the water.

7. Cover, cook on low for 3 hours. Let the cake cool in the pot.

Nutritional values per serving: net C 8g; P 7g; F 43g

Serve with whipped coconut cream and espresso.

---

5. Almond Cocoa Cake

Serves 6. Prep time: 15 minutes. Cooking: 3 hours on low.

List of Ingredients:

¾ cup butter, melted

1 ½ cups powdered sweetener

⅔ cup Dutch cocoa powder

⅓ cup ground almonds

Pinch of salt

3 large eggs

1 teaspoon vanilla

½ cup dark chocolate chips

Directions:

1. Line the crock-pot with aluminium foil and butter it.

2. In a bowl, mix all the ingredients.

3. Pour the batter into the buttered crock-pot.

4. Cover the pot with a paper towel to absorb the water.

5. Cover, cook on low for 3 hours.

Nutritional values per serving: net C 3g; P 6g; F 33g

Serve with whipped cream and espresso.

---

6. Chocolate Cheesecake

Serves 8. Prep time: 10 minutes. Cooking: 2.5 hours on high.

List of Ingredients:

3 cups cream cheese

Pinch of salt

3 eggs

1 cup powder sweetener of your choice, Swerve (or suitable substitute)

1 teaspoon vanilla extract

½ cup sugarless dark chocolate chips

Directions:

1. In a bowl, beat together the cream cheese, sweetener, and salt.

2. Add the eggs one at a time. Combine thoroughly.

3. Spread the cheesecake in a cake pan, which fits in the crock-pot you are using.

4. Melt the chocolate chips in a small pot and pour over the batter. Using a knife, swirl the chocolate through the batter.

5. Pour 2 cups of water in the crock-pot and set the cake pan inside. Attention: Careful the water does not exceed the level of the cake pan.

6. Cover the pot with a paper towel to absorb the water.

7. Cover, cook on high for 2.5 hours. Remove from the crock-pot and let it cool in the pan for 1 hour. Refrigerate.

Nutritional values per serving: net C 3g; P 8g; F 33g

Serve with whipped cream and espresso.

---

7. Crème Brûlée

Serves 6. Prep time: 10 minutes. Cooking: 2 hours on high.

List of Ingredients:

5 large egg yolks

6 Tablespoons sweetener, Erythritol

2 cups double cream

1 Bourbon vanilla pod, scraped

Pinch of salt

Directions:

1. In a bowl, beat the eggs and sweetener together.

2. Add the cream and vanilla. Whisk together.

3. Divide the mixture between 6 small ramekin dishes or one big dish.

4. Set them in the crock-pot and pour hot water around them - so the water reaches half way up the ramekins.

5. Cover, cook on high for 2 hours.

6. Take the dishes out, let them cool. Refrigerate for 6-8 hours.

Nutritional values per serving: net C 2g; P 2g; F 34g

Serve with whipped cream and espresso.

---

8. Peanut Butter & Chocolate Cake

Serves 12. Prep time: 10 minutes. Cooking: 4 hours on low.

List of Ingredients:

1 Tablespoon butter for greasing the crock-pot

2 cups almond flour

¾ cup sweetener of your choice

¼ cup coconut flakes

¼ cup whey protein powder

1 teaspoon baking powder

¼ teaspoon salt

¾ cup peanut butter, melted

4 large eggs

1 teaspoon vanilla extract

½ cup water

3 Tablespoons sugarless dark chocolate, melted

Directions:

1. Grease the crock-pot well.

2. In a bowl, mix the dry ingredients. Stir in the wet ingredients one at a time.

3. Spread about 2/3 of batter in the crock-pot, add half the chocolate. Swirl with a fork. Top up with the remaining batter and chocolate. Swirl again.

4. Cook on low for 4 hours. Switch off. Let it set covered for 30 minutes.

Nutritional values per serving: net C 5g; P 7g; F 21g

Serve with whipped cream and espresso.

---

9. Berry & Coconut Cake

Serves 8. Prep time: 10 minutes. Cooking: 2 hours on high.

List of Ingredients:

1 Tablespoon butter for greasing the crock

1 cup almond flour

¾ cup sweetener of your choice

1 teaspoon baking soda

¼ teaspoon salt

1 large egg, beaten with a fork

¼ cup coconut flour

¼ cup coconut milk

2 Tablespoons coconut oil

4 cups fresh or frozen blueberries and raspberries

Directions:

1. Butter the crock-pot well.

2. In a bowl, whisk the egg, coconut milk, and oil together.

3. Mix the dry ingredients. Slowly stir in the wet ingredients. Do not over mix.

4. Pour the batter in the crock-pot, spread evenly.

5. Spread the berries on top.

6. Cover, cook on high for 2 hours. Cool in the crock for 1-2 hours.

Nutritional values per serving: net C 7g; P 7g; F 17g

Serve with whipped cream and espresso.

10. Cocoa Pudding Cake

Serves 10. Prep time: 10 minutes. Cooking: 2.5-3 hours on low.

List of Ingredients:

1 Tablespoon butter for greasing the crock-pot

1 ½ cups ground almonds

¾ cup sweetener, Swerve (or a suitable substitute)

¾ cup cocoa powder

¼ cup whey protein

2 teaspoons baking powder

¼ teaspoon salt

4 large eggs

½ cup butter, melted

¾ cup full-fat cream

1 teaspoon vanilla extract

Directions:

1. Butter the crock-pot thoroughly.

2. In a bowl, whisk the dry ingredients together.

3. Stir in the melted butter, eggs, cream, and vanilla. Mix well.

4. Pour the batter into the crock-pot and spread evenly.

5. Cover, cook on low for 2½ to 3 hours. If preferred – more like pudding, cook cake shorter; more dry cake, cook longer.

6. Cool in the crock-pot for 30 minutes. Cut and serve.

Nutritional values per serving: net C 6.5g; P 7g; F 17g

Serve with whipped cream and espresso.

14-Day Ketogenic Diet Plan

This meal plan is for reference only. It does not consist of any dietary or medical advice.

The nutritional values under the respective recipes are only an approximation since the foods vary somewhat due to the individual circumstances of production.

All the recipes are suitable for breakfast, lunch, and dinner.

In order to make each and every meal in the slow cooker, you might need to have in your possession more than one slow cooking appliance.

For some meals, you can use leftovers (if you have any!) from some previous meals.

Do not use your slow cooker for reheating food.

Week 1

Monday

The Better Quiche Lorraine

Zucchini Lasagne with minced pork

Butcher Style Cabbage Rolls – Pork & Beef Version

Tuesday

Pepperoni Pizza with Meat Crust

Steak and Salsa

Stuffed Bell Peppers Dolma Style

Wednesday

Mocha Brownie

Zucchini & Spinach with Bacon

Mexican Flavour Chicken Soup

Thursday

Nut & Zucchini Bread

Slow BBQ-ish Ribs

Superb Oxtail Pot with Broccoli

Friday

Greek Style Frittata with Spinach and Feta Cheese

Mediterranean Meatloaf

Moorish Lamb Heart and Liver Soup

Saturday

Cheese & Cauliflower Bake

Two-meat Chilli

Mediterranean Fisherman One-Pot

Sunday

Ham & Cheese Broccoli Brunch Bowl

Beef Pot Roast with Turnips

Pork Shoulder Roast

Week 2

Monday

Greek Style Frittata with Spinach and Feta Cheese

Slightly addictive Pork Curry

Beef Meatball Soup

Tuesday

Zucchini & Spinach with Bacon

Whole Roasted Chicken

One-Pot Chicken and Green Beans

Wednesday

Chocolate Cheesecake

Pepperoni Pizza with Meat Crust

Seriously Delicious Lamb Stew

Thursday

The Better Quiche Lorraine

Greek Style Lamb Shanks

French Mint-Ball Veggie Soup

Friday

Peanut Butter & Chocolate Cake

Cheese & Cauliflower Bake

Veggie Chicken Soup

Saturday

Ham & Cheese Broccoli Brunch Bowl

Nut & Zucchini Bread

Chilli Beef Stew

Sunday

Pumpkin Nut Bread

Greek Mushroom Stew

Pot Roast Beef Brisket

Conclusion in few words

The Ketogenic diet is beneficial for your health and stamina.

Slow cooking is beneficial for your valet, time, and palate.

The combination of the two is the best thing you can do for your physical and mental well-being. Just try it and you will be an ardent follower for life.

Made in the USA
San Bernardino, CA
18 April 2018